God's Little Instruction Book

for Teens

David C. Cook

transforming lives together

GOD'S LITTLE INSTRUCTION BOOK FOR TEENS
Published by David C. Cook
4050 Lee Vance View
Colorado Springs, CO 80918 U.S.A.

David C. Cook Distribution Canada
55 Woodslee Avenue, Paris, Ontario, Canada N3L 3E5

David C. Cook U.K., Kingsway Communications
Eastbourne, East Sussex BN23 6NT, England

David C. Cook and the graphic circle C logo
are registered trademarks of Cook Communications Ministries.

Unless otherwise noted, all Scripture quotations are taken from the King James
Version of the Bible. (Public Domain.) Scripture quotations marked NIV are
taken from the *New International Version*®. *NIV*®. Copyright © 1973, 1978,
1984 by International Bible Society. Used by permission of Zondervan. All
rights reserved; TLB are taken from *The Living Bible*, copyright © 1971, Tyndale
House Publishers, Wheaton, IL 60189. Used by permission; NASB are taken from
the *New American Standard Bible*, © Copyright 1960, 1995 by The Lockman
Foundation. Used by permission; AMP are taken from *The Amplified Bible*.
Copyright © 1954, 1987 by The Lockman Foundation. Used by permission.

ISBN 978-1-56292-799-8

© 1998 David C. Cook

Cover Photo: Stockbyte

Printed in the United States of America
First Edition 1998

7 8 9 10 11 12 13 14 15

083010

Get Fired Up!

You haven't quite made it all the way into the world of adults, but you're almost there—and you sure aren't a kid anymore!

New issues and challenges face you every day. Where do you turn for advice? How do you get fired up when you're feeling a little knocked down?

God's Little Instruction Book for Teens is a great source of wisdom and encouragement to help you meet life head on—not just get by—with poise, style, integrity, and faith.

Take the powerful quotes and scriptures found in this handy little book to heart. You will be well on your way to making an incredible difference in your world!

Many recieve advice; only the wise profit by it

Pride only breeds quarrels, but wisdom
is found in those who take advice.

— Proverbs 13:10 NIV

The only way to
have a friend
is to be one.

A man that hath friends must
shew himself friendly.

— Proverbs 18:24

The world wants
your best, but God
wants your all.

"Thou shalt love the Lord thy God
with all thy heart, and with all
thy soul, and with all thy mind."

— Matthew 22:37

A Christian must keep the faith, but not to himself.

"Go ye into all the world, and preach the gospel to every creature."

— Mark 16:15

No horse gets anywhere
until he is harnessed.
No life ever grows great
until it is focused,
dedicated, disciplined.

In a race, everyone runs but only one person
gets first prize. . . . To win the contest you must
deny yourselves many things that would keep you
from doing your best.

— 1 Corinthians 9:24-25 TLB

I have never been
hurt by anything
I didn't say.

Don't talk so much. You keep
putting your foot in your mouth.
Be sensible and turn off the flow!

— Proverbs 10:19 TLB

We too often love things and use people, when we should be using things and loving people.

Be devoted to one another in brotherly love. Honor one another above yourselves.

— Romans 12:10 NIV

When you flee temptations, don't leave a forwarding address.

Now flee from youthful lusts and
pursue righteousness . . . with those who
call on the Lord from a pure heart.

— 2 Timothy 2:22 NASB

Whatever you dislike
in another person,
take care to correct
in yourself.

"Why do you look at the speck of sawdust
in your brother's eye and pay no attention
to the plank in your own eye?"

— Matthew 7:3 NIV

Shoot for the moon.
Even if you miss it
you will land among
the stars.

Aim for perfection.

— 2 Corinthians 13:11 NIV

The secret of
success is to do
the common things
uncommonly well.

Seest thou a man diligent in his business?
he shall stand before kings;
he shall not stand before mean men.

— Proverbs 22:29

Definition of status:
Buying something you
don't need with money
you don't have to impress
people you don't like.

They do all their deeds to be noticed by men.

— Matthew 23:5 NASB

16

I like the dreams of the future better than the history of the past.

Remember ye not the former things,
neither consider the things of old.
Behold, I will do a new thing.

— Isaiah 43:18-19

The way to get to the top is to get off your bottom.

How long will you lie down, O sluggard?
When will you arise from your sleep?

— Proverbs 6:9 NASB

You are only what
you are when no
one is looking.

Not with eye-service, as men-pleasers;
but as the servants of Christ, doing
the will of God from the heart.

— Ephesians 6:6

There are times when
silence is golden,
other times it is
just plain yellow.

To every thing there is a season . . . a
time to keep silence, and a time to speak.

— Ecclesiastes 3:1-7

A true friend never gets in your way unless you happen to be going down.

If one falls down, his friend can
help him up. But pity the man who
falls and has no one to help him up!

— Ecclesiastes 4:10 NIV

Every job is a self-portrait of the person who does it. Autograph your work with excellence.

Daniel was preferred above the presidents and princes, because an excellent spirit was in him.

— Daniel 6:3

The best things in life are **not** free.

Forasmuch as ye know that ye
were not redeemed with corruptible
things, as silver and gold . . . but with
the precious blood of Christ, as of a
lamb without blemish and without spot.

— 1 Peter 1:18-19

You can lead
a boy to college,
but you cannot
make him think.

It is senseless to pay tuition to educate
a rebel who has no heart for truth.

— Proverbs 17:16 TLB

If a man cannot be a Christian in the place where he is, he cannot be a Christian anywhere.

Don't work hard only when your master is watching and then shirk when he isn't looking; work hard and with gladness all the time, as though working for Christ, doing the will of God with all your hearts.

— Ephesians 6:6–7 TLB

Don't ask God for what
you think is good;
ask Him for what He
thinks is good for you.

"After this manner therefore pray ye . . .
Thy kingdom come. Thy will be done
in earth, as it is in heaven."

— Matthew 6:9-10

Opportunities are seldom labeled.

Seek, and ye shall find; knock,
and it shall be opened unto you.

— Matthew 7:7

The wise does at once what the fool does at last.

He that gathereth in summer is a wise son: but he that sleepeth in harvest is a son that causeth shame.

— Proverbs 10:5

Nothing great was ever achieved without enthusiasm.

The joy of the Lord is your strength.

— Nehemiah 8:10

Trust in yourself and
you are doomed to
disappointment; but trust
in God, and you are
never to be confounded
in time or eternity.

It is better to take refuge in
the Lord than to trust in man.

— Psalm 118:8 NIV

Don't be discouraged; everyone who got where he is, started where he was.

Though your beginning was insignificant,
yet your end will increase greatly.

— Job 8:7 NASB

Maturity doesn't
come with age; it
comes with acceptance
of responsibility.

When I was a child, I spake as a child,
I understood as a child, I thought
as a child: but when I became a man,
I put away childish things.

— 1 Corinthians 13:11

The man who wins may have been counted out several times, but he didn't hear the referee.

Though a righteous man falls seven times, he rises again.

— Proverbs 24:16 NIV

The happiest people
don't necessarily have
the best of everything.
They just make the
best of everything.

I have learned, in whatsoever state I am,
therewith to be content. I can do all things
through Christ which strengtheneth me.

— Philippians 4:11,13

Keep company with good men and good men you will imitate.

Iron sharpeneth iron; so a man sharpeneth
the countenance of his friend.

— Proverbs 27:17

Learn by experience— preferably other people's.

All these things happened to them as
examples—as object lessons to us—
to warn us against doing the same things.

— 1 Corinthians 10:11 TLB

Many men have too much will power. It's **won't** power they lack.

A man without self-control is as defenseless
as a city with broken-down walls.

— Proverbs 25:28 TLB

It's not hard
to make decisions
when you know what
your values are.

Daniel purposed in his heart that
he would not defile himself.

— Daniel 1:8

Conquer yourself
rather than
the world.

Encourage the young men
to be self-controlled.

— Titus 2:6 NIV

I am only one; but still
I am one. I cannot do
everything, but still I can do
something; I will not refuse
to do the something I can do.

Under his direction the whole body is fitted together

perfectly, and each part in its

own special way helps the other parts.

— Ephesians 4:16 TLB

Politeness goes far, yet costs nothing.

A kind man benefits himself.

— Proverbs 11:17 NIV

We should behave
to our friends as we
would wish our friends
to behave to us.

"As ye would that men should do to you,
do ye also to them likewise."

— Luke 6:31

Who ceases to be a friend, never was one.

This people honors Me with their lips,
but their heart is far away from Me.

— Mark 7:6 NASB

Character is what you are in the dark.

The integrity of the upright
shall guide them.

— Proverbs 11:3

Adversity
causes some men
to break; others
to break records.

If thou faint in the day of adversity,
thy strength is small.

— Proverbs 24:10

Learn to say "No";
it will be of more
use to you than to be
able to read Latin.

Just say a simple yes or no,
so that you will not sin.

— James 5:12 TLB

A man who wants
to lead the orchestra
must turn his
back on the crowd.

Wherefore come out from among them, and be
ye separate, saith the Lord, and touch not
the unclean thing; and I will receive you.

— 2 Corinthians 6:17

Men are alike in
their promises. It is
only in their deeds
that they differ.

Many a man claims to have unfailing love,
but a faithful man who can find?

— Proverbs 20:6 NIV

Don't cross your bridges until

you get to them.

We spend our lives

defeating ourselves

crossing bridges

we never get to.

Don't be anxious about tomorrow.
God will take care of your tomorrow too.
Live one day at a time.

— Matthew 6:34 TLB

He that has
learned to obey
will know how
to command.

The wise in heart accept commands,
but a chattering fool comes to ruin.

— Proverbs 10:8 NIV

You must have long-range goals to keep you from being frustrated by short-range failures.

Let us fix our eyes on Jesus, the author
and perfecter of our faith, who for
the joy set before him endured the cross,
scorning its shame, and sat down at the right
hand of the throne of God.

— Hebrews 12:2 NIV

Clear your mind of can't.

I can do all things through Christ
which strengtheneth me.

— Philippians 4:13

The future
belongs to those
who believe in the beauty
of their dreams.

"Anything is possible if you have faith."

— Mark 9:23 TLB

The future belongs
to those who see
possibilities before
they become obvious.

The vision is yet for an appointed time . . .
it will surely come, it will not tarry.

— Habakkuk 2:3

When I was a young man
I observed that nine out
of ten things I did were
failures. I didn't want
to be a failure, so I did
ten times more work.

He becometh poor that dealeth
with a slack hand: but the hand
of the diligent maketh rich.

— Proverbs 10:4

To recognize opportunity is the difference between success and failure.

Make the most of every opportunity.

— Colossians 4:5 NIV

Jumping to conclusions
is not half as good
an exercise as digging
for facts.

Study to shew thyself approved unto God,
a workman that needeth not to be ashamed,
rightly dividing the word of truth.

— 2 Timothy 2:15

The most valuable of
all talents is that of
never using two words
when one will do.

In the multitude of words there wanteth not sin:
but he that refraineth his lips is wise.

— Proverbs 10:19

Laziness is often mistaken for patience.

Let us lay aside every weight, and the sin which doth so easily beset us, and let us run with patience the race that is set before us.

— Hebrews 12:1

One-half the trouble

of this life can be

traced to saying "yes"

too quick, and not

saying "no" soon enough.

Seest thou a man that is hasty in his words?

there is more hope of a fool than of him.

— Proverbs 29:20

I would rather fail in the cause that someday will triumph than triumph in a cause that someday will fail.

Now thanks be unto God, which always causeth us to triumph in Christ.

— 2 Corinthians 2:14

Carve your name on hearts and not on marble.

The only letter I need is you yourselves!
They can see that you are a letter from
Christ, written by us. . . . not one
carved on stone, but in human hearts.

— 2 Corinthians 3:2,3 TLB

A knowledge of the Bible without a college course is more valuable than a college course without the Bible.

All scripture is given by inspiration of God,
and is profitable for doctrine, for reproof, for
correction, for instruction in righteousness: that
the man of God may be perfect,
thoroughly furnished unto all good works.

— 2 Timothy 3:16-17

Little minds are tamed
and subdued by
misfortune; but great
minds rise above them.

A just man falleth seven times,
and riseth up again.

— Proverbs 24:16

There is no
poverty that
can overtake
diligence.

He becometh poor that dealeth
with a slack hand: but the hand
of the diligent maketh rich.

— Proverbs 10:4

Never despair;
but if you do,
work on in despair.

Be strong and do not give up,
for your work will be rewarded.

— 2 Chronicles 15:7 NIV

Y ou can accomplish
more in one hour
with God than one
lifetime without Him.

"With God all things are possible."

— Matthew 19:26

If you don't stand
for something,
you'll fall
for anything!

If you do not stand firm in your faith,
you will not stand at all.

— Isaiah 7:9 NIV

The difference
between ordinary
and extraordinary is
that little extra.

Whatsoever thy hand findeth to do,
do it with thy might.

— Ecclesiastes 9:10

Man cannot discover new oceans unless he has the courage to lose sight of the shore.

Peter got out of the boat, and walked on the water and came toward Jesus.

— Matthew 14:29 NASB

Fads come and go;
wisdom and
character go
on forever.

O my son, be wise and stay in God's paths.

— Proverbs 23:19 TLB

Perseverance is a great
element of success; if you
only knock long enough
and loud enough at
the gate, you are sure
to wake up somebody.

"Ask, and it shall be given you;
seek, and ye shall find; knock,
and it shall be opened unto you."

— Luke 11:9

Consider the postage
stamp: its usefulness
consists in the ability
to stick to one thing
till it gets there.

I have fought a good fight, I have
finished my course, I have kept the faith.

— 2 Timothy 4:7

It needs more skill
than I can tell to
play the second
fiddle well.

He that is greatest among
you shall be your servant.

— Matthew 23:11

A man never discloses his own character so clearly as when he describes another's.

A good man out of the good treasure
of the heart bringeth forth good things:
and an evil man out of the evil treasure
bringeth forth evil things.

— Matthew 12:35

The greatest use
of life is to spend
it for something
that will outlast it.

Store up for yourselves treasures in heaven,
where moth and rust do not destroy, and where
thieves do not break in and steal.

— Matthew 6:20 NIV

Every man's work, whether
it be literature, or music,
or pictures, or architecture, or
anything else, is always
a portrait of himself.

As in water face reflects face, so
the heart of man reflects man.

— Proverbs 27:19 NASB

What we do on some great
occasion will probably depend
on what we already are;
and what we are will
be the result of previous
years of self-discipline.

I keep under my body, and
bring it into subjection.
— 1 Corinthians 9:27

Our deeds determine us, as much as we determine our deeds.

Even a child is known by his actions, by whether his conduct is pure and right.

— Proverbs 20:11 NIV

What you do
speaks so loud
that I cannot hear
what you say.

Show me your faith without deeds, and
I will show you my faith by what I do.

— James 2:18 NIV

All virtue is summed up in dealing justly.

He hath shewed thee, O man, what is good;
and what doth the LORD require of thee,
but to do justly, and to love mercy,
and to walk humbly with thy God?

— Micah 6:8

No matter what a man's past may have been, his future is spotless.

Forgetting those things which are behind, and reaching forth unto those things which are before.

— Philippians 3:13

One of Life's
great rules is this:
The more you give,
the more you get.

The liberal soul shall be made fat:
and he that watereth shall
be watered also himself.

— Proverbs 11:25

Everything comes to him who hustles while he waits.

We do not want you to become lazy, but to imitate those who through faith and patience inherit what has been promised.

— Hebrews 6:12 NIV

A well-trained memory
is one that permits
you to forget
everything that isn't
worth remembering.

Whatsoever things are true, whatsoever
things are honest, whatsoever things are
just . . . if there be any virtue, and if
there be any praise, think on these things.
— Philippians 4:8

Defeat is not the worst of failures. Not to have tried is the true failure.

Be strong and of a good courage;
be not afraid, neither be thou dismayed:
for the Lord thy God is with thee
whithersoever thou goest.

— Joshua 1:9

Unless you try to
do something beyond
what you have already
mastered, you will
never grow.

Reaching forth unto those things which are
before, I press toward the mark for the prize of
the high calling of God in Christ Jesus.

— Philippians 3:13-14

I don't know the secret to success, but the key to failure is to try to please everyone.

Am I now trying to win the approval of men, or of God?

— Galatians 1:10 NIV

Kites rise highest

against the wind,

not with it.

When the way is rough, your patience has a
chance to grow. So let it grow, and don't
try to squirm out of your problems.

— James 1:3-4 TLB

The secret of success is to be like a duck— smooth and unruffled on top, but paddling furiously underneath.

I laboured more abundantly than they all: yet not I, but the grace of God which was with me.

— 1 Corinthians 15:10

The cheerful man will do more in the same time, will do it better, will preserve it longer, than the sad or sullen.

When a man is gloomy, everything seems to go wrong; when he is cheerful, everything seems right!

— Proverbs 15:15 TLB

Money is a good servant but a bad master.

The rich ruleth over the poor, and the
borrower is servant to the lender.

— Proverbs 22:7

No plan is worth the paper it is printed on unless it starts you doing something.

Be ye doers of the word, and not hearers only, deceiving your own selves.

— James 1:22

Life is a coin. You can spend it any way you wish, but you can spend it only once.

As it is appointed unto men once to die, but after this the judgment.

— Hebrews 9:27

Only passions,
great passions, can
elevate the soul
to great things.

What things soever ye desire, when
ye pray, believe that ye receive
them, and ye shall have them.

— Mark 11:24

Failures want
pleasing methods,
successes want
pleasing results.

No discipline seems pleasant at the time,
but painful. Later on, however, it produces
a harvest of righteousness and peace
for those who have been trained by it.

— Hebrews 12:11 NIV

Once a word has been allowed to escape, it cannot be recalled.

Let no corrupt communication proceed out of your mouth, but that which is good to the use of edifying, that it may minister grace unto the hearers.

— Ephesians 4:29

Most of the things
worth doing in the world
had been declared
impossible before
they were done.

"With God all things are possible."

— Matthew 19:26

Obstacles are those
frightful things you
see when you take your
eyes off the goal.

So Peter . . . walked on the water toward Jesus.
But when he looked around at the high waves, he
was terrified and began to sink.

Matthew 14:29–30 TLB

A good reputation
is more valuable
than money.

A good name is rather to be
chosen than great riches.

— Proverbs 22:1

An error doesn't
become a mistake
until you refuse
to correct it.

He who heeds discipline shows the
way to life, but whoever ignores
correction leads others astray.

— Proverbs 10:17 NIV

Hating people is like burning down your own house to get rid of a rat.

If ye bite and devour one another, take heed
that ye be not consumed one of another.

— Galatians 5:15

Laughter is the
sun that drives
winter from the
human face.

A merry heart maketh a cheerful
countenance: but by sorrow of
the heart the spirit is broken.

— Proverbs 15:13

Good nature begets smiles, smiles beget friends, and friends are better than a fortune.

The light in the eyes (of him whose heart is joyful) rejoices the heart of others.

— Proverbs 15:30 AMP

No person was ever
honored for what he
received. Honor has
been the reward
for what he gave.

The **righteous** give without sparing.

— Proverbs 21:26 NIV

The difference between the right word and the almost right word is the difference between lightning and the lightning bug.

A word fitly spoken is like apples of gold in pictures of silver.

— Proverbs 25:11

This world belongs to
the man who is wise
enough to change
his mind in the
presence of facts.

Whoever heeds correction
gains understanding.
— Proverbs 15:32 NIV

Do not remove
a fly from your
friend's forehead
with a hatchet.

Reprove, rebuke, exhort, with
great patience and instruction.

— 2 Timothy 4:2 NASB

Every calling
is great when
greatly pursued.

I press toward the mark for the prize of
the high calling of God in Christ Jesus.

— Philippians 3:14

Treat everybody alike,
no matter from what station
in life he comes . . . really
great men and women are
those who are natural, frank,
and honest with everyone with
whom they come into contact.

Don't show favoritism.

— James 2:1 NIV

'Tis better to
be alone, than in
bad company.

Do not be misled: "Bad company
corrupts good character."

— 1 Corinthians 15:33 NIV

The rotten
apple spoils
his companion.

He that walketh with wise men shall be wise: but

a companion of fools shall be destroyed.

— Proverbs 13:20

Patience is
bitter but its
fruit is sweet.

Ye have need of patience, that,
after ye have done the will of God,
ye might receive the promise.

— Hebrews 10:36

Motivation is when your dreams put on work clothes.

Whatever you do, work at it with all your heart,
as working for the Lord, not for men.

— Colossians 3:23 NIV

Not only to say the right
thing in the right place,
but far more difficult, to
leave unsaid the wrong thing
at the tempting moment.

Self-control means controlling the tongue!
A quick retort can ruin everything.

— Proverbs 13:3 TLB

School seeks to get you ready for examination; life gives the finals.

Examine yourselves to see whether you
are in the faith; test yourselves.

— 2 Corinthians 13:5 NIV

Diligence is
the mother of
good fortune.

The plans of the diligent lead to profit.

— Proverbs 21:5 NIV

The road to success is dotted with many tempting parking places.

Let us lay aside every weight, and the sin which
doth so easily beset us, and let us run with
patience the race that is set before us.

— Hebrews 12:1

When you are laboring for others let it be with the same zeal as if it were for yourself.

Each of you should look not only
to your own interests, but
also to the interests of others.

— Philippians 2:4 NIV

The Bible knows nothing
of a hierarchy of labor.
No work is degrading.
If it ought to be done,
then it is good work.

To rejoice in his labour;
this is the gift of God.

— Ecclesiastes 5:19

The ripest peach is highest on the tree.

Let us not become weary in doing good,
for at the proper time we will reap
a harvest if we do not give up.

— Galatians 6:9 NIV

When you do the things
you have to do when you
have to do them, the day will
come when you can do the
things you want to do when
you want to do them.

He becometh poor that dealeth
with a slack hand: but the hand
of the diligent maketh rich.

— Proverbs 10:4

A man without mirth is like a wagon without springs, he is jolted disagreeably by every pebble in the road.

A merry heart doeth good like a medicine:
but a broken spirit drieth the bones.

— Proverbs 17:22

The two most important
words: "Thank you."
The most important word:
"We."
The least important word:
"I."

Don't be selfish. . . . Be humble, thinking
of others as better than yourself.

— Philippians 2:3 ᴛʟʙ

Here's the key to success and the key to failure: we become what we think about.

Whatsoever things are true, whatsoever things are honest . . . if there be any virtue, and if there be any praise, think on these things.

— Philippians 4:8

Always bear in mind
that your own resolution
to success is more
important than any
other one thing.

The Lord God will help me; therefore
shall I not be confounded: therefore
have I set my face like a flint, and
I know that I shall not be ashamed.

— Isaiah 50:7

Triumph is
just "umph"
added to try.

Whatsoever thy hand findeth to do,
do it with thy might.

— Ecclesiastes 9:10

A goal properly set
is halfway reached.

The LORD answered me, and said, Write the
vision, and make it plain upon tables,
that he may run that readeth it.

— Habakkuk 2:2

I think the one lesson
I have learned is that
there is no substitute
for paying attention.

We ought to give the more earnest heed
to the things which we have heard,
lest at any time we should let them slip.

— Hebrews 2:1

A good listener
is not only popular
everywhere, but
after a while he
knows something.

The ear that heareth the reproof
of life abideth among the wise.

— Proverbs 15:31

When you were born, you
cried and the world rejoiced.
Live your life in such a
manner that when you die the
world cries and you rejoice.

The memory of the righteous
will be a blessing.

— Proverbs 10:7 NIV

Success is never final;
failure is never fatal;
it is courage
that counts.

Be of good courage, and he shall strengthen your
heart, all ye that hope in the LORD.

— Psalm 31:24

I count him braver
who overcomes his
desires than him who
conquers his enemies; for
the hardest victory is
the victory over self.

I beat my body and make it my slave.

— 1 Corinthians 9:27 NIV

Vision is the world's most desperate need. There are no hopeless situations, only people who think hopelessly.

Where there is no vision, the people perish.

— Proverbs 29:18

People are lonely because they build walls instead of bridges.

You should be like one big happy family . . . loving one another with tender hearts and humble minds.

— 1 Peter 3:8 TLB

Forgiveness means giving up your right to punish another.

When you stand praying, if you hold anything against anyone, forgive him, so that your Father in heaven may forgive you your sins.

— Mark 11:25 NIV

The most important single ingredient in the formula of success is knowing how to get along with people.

See that no one pays back evil for evil,
but always try to do good to each
other and to everyone else.

— 1 Thessalonians 5:15 TLB

Everyone thinks of
changing the world,
but no one thinks
of changing himself.

"Unless you change and become
like little children, you will
never enter the kingdom of heaven."

— Matthew 18:3 NIV

Courage is
resistance to fear,
mastery of fear—
not absence of fear.

Yea, though I walk through the
valley of the shadow of death, I will
fear no evil: for thou art with me;
thy rod and thy staff they comfort me.

— Psalm 23:4

Prayer is an invisible tool which is wielded in a visible world.

The weapons of our warfare are not
carnal, but mighty through God to
the pulling down of strong holds.
— 2 Corinthians 10:4

Money is like
an arm or leg:
use it or lose it.

"To him who has will more be given . . .
and he will have great plenty;
but from him who has not, even the
little he has will be taken away."

— Matthew 13:12 TLB

In trying times, don't quit trying.

The righteous also shall hold on his way,
and he that hath clean hands
shall be stronger and stronger.

— Job 17:9

Let us not say, "Every man is the architect of his own fortune"; but let us say, "Every man is the architect of his own character."

Till I die I will not remove mine integrity from me. My righteousness I hold fast, and will not let it go: my heart shall not reproach me so long as I live.

— Job 27:5-6

It is impossible for that man to despair who remembers that his Helper is omnipotent.

I will lift up my eyes to the mountains;
from whence shall my help come?
My help comes from the LORD,
who made heaven and earth.

— Psalm 121:1-2 NASB

Service is
nothing but love
in work clothes.

The more lowly your service
to others, the greater you are.
To be the greatest, be a servant.

— Matthew 23:11 TLB

Those who have
done nothing in life
are not qualified to be
the judge of those who
have done little.

"Judge not, and ye shall not
be judged: condemn not, and
ye shall not be condemned."

— Luke 6:37

People, places, and things were never meant to give us life. God alone is the author of a fulfilling life.

"I am come that they might have life, and that they might have it more abundantly."

— John 10:10

COMMON COURTESIES FOR TEENS

"Treat others the same way
you want them to treat you."

—Luke 6:31 NASB

Always say "thank you"

when you receive a favor,

and say "excuse me" or

"pardon me" when needing

to interrupt a discussion.

Always knock and ask permission before entering someone's room.

Don't put your feet up on furniture. Feet do not enhance the look of the desk or the table.

Always RSVP
promptly to
every invitation
you receive.

Return anything
borrowed on time,
and in good or better
condition than received.

Be on time for appointments; leave on time, too, for nothing is more boring than someone who overstays his welcome.

When you dial a wrong number, say, "I'm sorry, excuse me"—instead of slamming down the receiver in the other person's ear.

Acknowledgments

Publius Syrus (5,100), R. W. Emerson (6,29,80), Jim Patrick (8), H. E. Fosdick (9,102), Calvin Coolidge (10,105), Sprat (13), Les Brown (14), John Rockefeller, Jr. (15), Dr. Eugene Swearingen (16,18), Thomas Jefferson (17,58), Robert C. Edward (19), Ed Cole (20,32,140), Arnold Glasow (21), Kin Hubbard (24), Henry Ward Beecher (25,123), John A. Shedd (27,37), Dwight L. Moody (30,44), H. E. Jansen (33), Roy Disney (38), Descartes (39), Helen Keller (40), Seneca (41), Aristotle (42,81,133), William A. Ward (45), Charles H. Spurgeon (46,62), Moliere (48), Bob Bales (49), Solon (50), Charles C. Noble (51), Samuel Johnson (52,146), Eleanor Roosevelt (53), John Sculley (54), George Bernard Shaw (55), Benjamin Franklin (60,112), Woodrow Wilson (61), William Lyon Phelps (63), Washington Irving (64), Terence (66), Henry Wadsworth Longfellow (72), Josh Billings (73), Jean Paul Richter (75), William James (76), Samuel Butler (77), H. P. Liddon (78), George Elliot (78), John R. Rice (82), William H. Danforth (83,93,110), Thomas Edison (84), Orlando Battista (85,101), George Woodberry (86), Ronald E. Osborn (87), Bill Cosby (88), Winston Churchill (89,132), Thomas Carlyle (91), Bacon (92), Lillian Dickson (92), Denis Diderot (95), Earl Nightingale (96,125), Horace (97), Louis D. Brandeis (98), Hannah More (99), Victor Hugo (103), David Dunn (104), Mark Twain (106,139), Roy L. Smith (107), Chinese Proverb (108), Oliver Wendell Holmes (109), George Washington (111), Parks Robinson (114), George Sala (115), Say (116), Cervantes (117), Ben Patterson (120), James Riley (121), Zig Ziglar (122,128), Abraham Lincoln (126), Diane Sawyer (129), Wilson Mizner (130), Winefred Newman (134), Joseph Newton (135), Dennis Rainey (136), Theodore Roosevelt (137), Leo Tolstoy (138), Henry Ford (141), George Boardman (143), Jeremy Taylor (144), Gary Smalley & John Trent (147).